THE
Future
Architect's
HANDBOOK

Barbara Beck, ARCHITECT

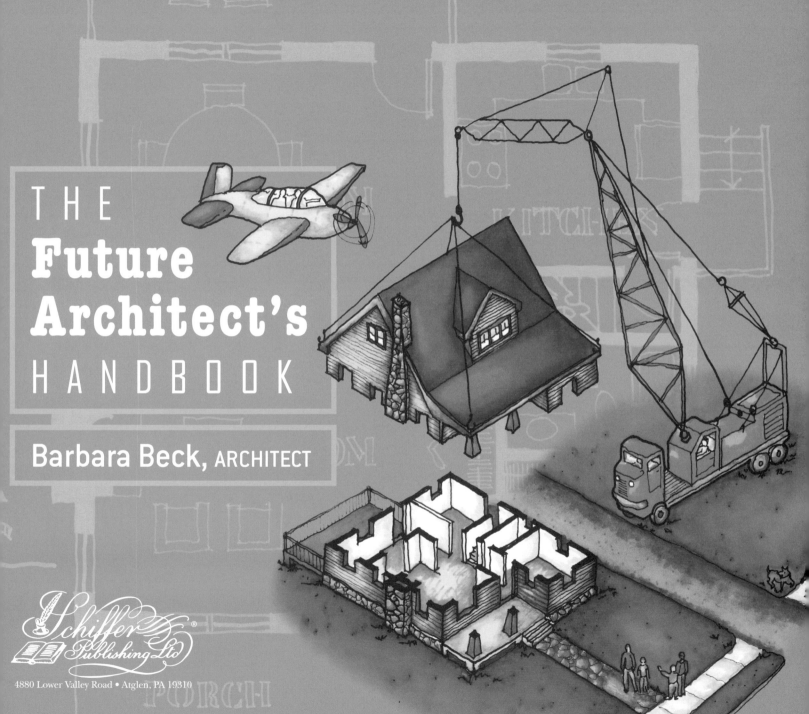

THE
Future
Architect's
HANDBOOK

Barbara Beck, ARCHITECT

Schiffer Publishing Ltd®

4880 Lower Valley Road • Atglen, PA 19310

Designed by Justin Watkinson
Type set in ITC American Typewriter/Conduit OSITC

ISBN: 978-0-7643-4676-7
Printed in China

Published by Schiffer Publishing, Ltd.
4880 Lower Valley Road
Atglen, PA 19310
Phone: (610) 593-1777; Fax: (610) 593-2002
E-mail: Info@schifferbooks.com

For our complete selection of fine books on this and related subjects, please visit our website at www.schifferbooks.com. You may also write for a free catalog.

This book may be purchased from the publisher. Please try your bookstore first.

We are always looking for people to write books on new and related subjects. If you have an idea for a book, please contact us at proposals@schifferbooks.com.

Schiffer Publishing's titles are available at special discounts for bulk purchases for sales promotions or premiums. Special editions, including personalized covers, corporate imprints, and excerpts can be created in large quantities for special needs. For more information, contact the publisher.

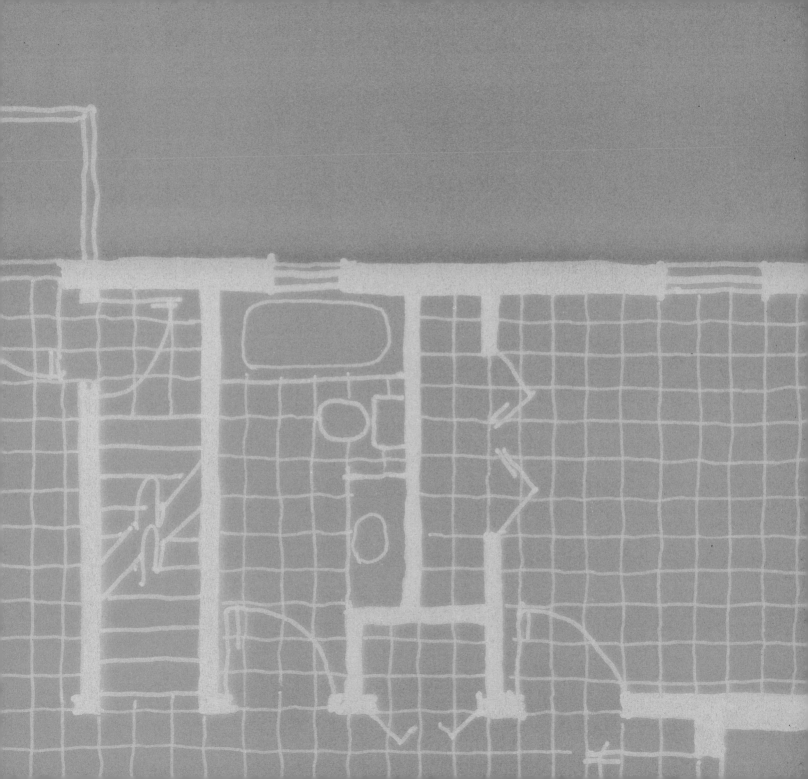

CONTENTS

ACKNOWLEDGMENTS

Thanks to my husband, Richard Compton, for his support;
To Janet Aljunaidi, who read and re-read the manuscript;
To fellow architect and friend, Jean Johnson Rose,
who gave amazing architectural suggestions;
To Gail Johnson, writing support extraordinaire;
To Lucille Bower, who told me not to give up;
And to my Mom and Dad, who urged me to follow my dreams.

CHAPTER ONE

Architecture and Architects

Buildings are where we work, play, and study.
Buildings shelter us from weather.
Buildings provide a place to live.

Architecture is the art and science of building. The art of architecture means a building captivates our senses and is pleasing to see. The science of architecture is how a building is physically constructed.

The word *architect* comes from the Greek word *architektón,* which means master builder, but an architect is not a builder. An architect is in charge of the building team.

An architect is a bit like a fashion designer. A fashion designer has an idea for a piece of clothing—what it should look like, what color and material it should be, and how it should fit. The designer draws a pattern that a dressmaker or tailor uses to sew the clothes.

In a similar way, an architect has an idea how a building should look, how it should work, and how it should fit in its surroundings. He or she then creates drawings that are used as patterns for construction.

In this book, we will study the architectural drawings for one specific building: Aaron's house. When you see the drawings, you may notice that some of the lines are crooked and the letters are squiggly. Drawings, like people, are not perfect. They have personality. As long as a drawing conveys an idea, it has value. Never be afraid to draw.

Aaron is an architect. When he was little, he liked to draw, and his favorite things to draw were houses. When Aaron wasn't drawing houses, he was reading about castles and building skyscrapers with his bedroom furniture. Did you ever do anything like that?

Aaron's older sister, Margie, is also an architect. She didn't build furniture skyscrapers when she was little, she built castles. When she saw Aaron's creations, she told him he should become an architect like her.

In college, Aaron studied art, math, and engineering. After graduation, he worked for several years. He learned about safety, building codes, zoning regulations, construction methods, mechanical and electrical systems, and even how much a building costs to build. Finally, he knew enough to pass a national architectural test. Now Aaron is an architect like Margie.

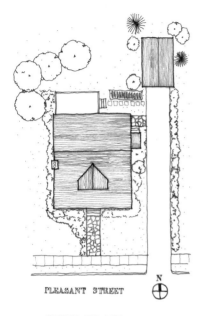

PLEASANT STREET   N

SITE PLAN

DECK

DINING ROOM   KITCHEN

BATH

LIVING ROOM

BEDROOM

PORCH

FLOOR PLAN

These are the drawings for Aaron's house. They are the same ones every architect everywhere creates. They are the *site plan*, the *floor plan*, the *section*, and the *elevation*.

Let's go through these drawings one-by-one to see how Aaron created something as important as a house. But first, we need to understand more about what makes up a building.

SECTION   A

ELEVATION

CHAPTER TWO

Building Components

Every building is different, yet in many ways, is the same as every other building. They all share certain *components*. These are the *wall, doors and windows, roof, floor,* and the *structure.*

The first thing you see when approaching a building is the outside *wall. Exterior* walls are like a person's skin. They enclose and protect the building's important inner workings. Walls can be made of stone, concrete, brick, wood, and even glass.

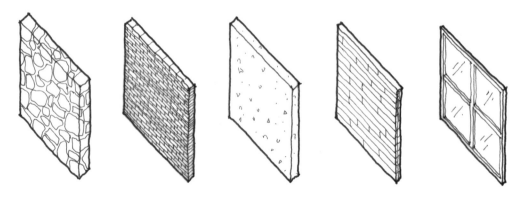

Sunshine warms walls just as it warms our skin. Think about a house in the desert. It has thick walls to keep out the intense sun and heat. In a cold climate, however, we want to keep the heat in, so that house is insulated like a winter coat.

What about where you live? Which is more important—cooling off or getting warm? Is the weather usually wet or dry? The answers to these questions determine what clothing you wear. They also helped shape your house.

Doors and *windows* are the second component you see when looking at a building. Like your eyes, nose, and mouth, they are openings in the building's skin. They add beauty and personality to a building, let people pass from outside to inside and from room to room, and allow light and air inside.

Large windows give the impression of being outside, while small windows make us feel enclosed. The shape of a window can make us feel like we belong to another time and place.

The third building component is the *roof*. A building's roof protects the interior from rain, snow, and harsh sunshine the same way a hat protects our head. There are many different roofs, just as there are many different hats. The type of roof used depends on climate, surrounding buildings, tradition, and the visual image desired.

When you were little, did you draw a house that looked like this?

If you did, you were drawing a gabled roof, the most common roof for houses in much of the world.

A shed roof is often used for basic shelter. Two shed roofs leaning against each other create a gable.

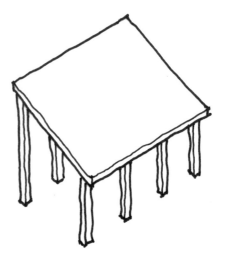

A hipped roof was used on the Prairie style houses of the famous architect, Frank Lloyd Wright.

Gambrel roofs are sometimes found on barns.

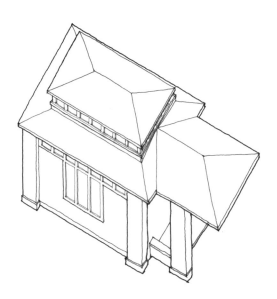

The fourth component is the *floor*, the horizontal plane that we stand and walk on. Floors sit on the ground, on top of walls, or are supported by walls. Floors have the important function of tying walls in place. They are also part of the next component.

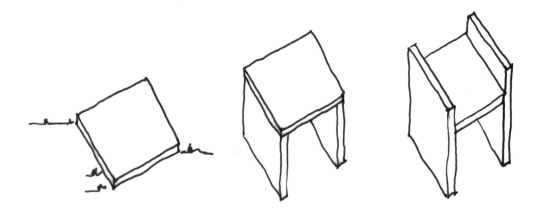

The fifth building component is the *structure*. Structure is like a person's skeleton. Our skeletons hold us upright and give us our unique shape. The structure does the same for a building, whether it's the Eiffel Tower or the Parthenon.

The structure also keeps a building's occupants safe from forces of gravity, strong winds, and earthquakes.

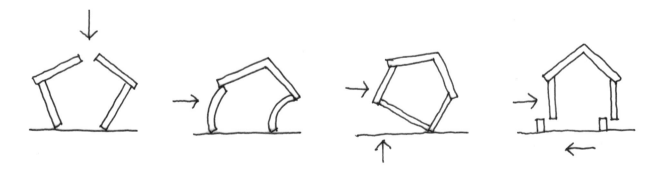

Structure can be made of wood, brick, stone, steel, or concrete.

All of these physical components worked together to shape Aaron's house.

CHAPTER THREE

The Site Plan

Before designing his house, Aaron needed to decide where to live. Sometimes it takes months to find the perfect location, but Aaron was lucky. His sister, Margie, lives in a friendly neighborhood where there was an empty lot. That's Aaron's house on the left, with his dog, Artemis, in the front yard.

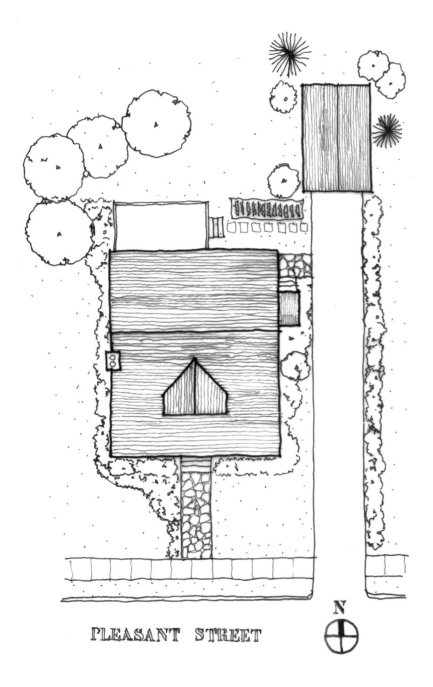

PLEASANT STREET

N

SITE PLAN

The *site* is the land on which a building sits. Aaron's site is his front yard and back yard and everything on his property. A *site plan* is a view from above, the one you would get if you were a bird flying over Aaron's property.

This is Aaron's site plan. Notice the difference between the previous drawing and this one. The site plan shows the exact placement of everything on Aaron's property. Because of that, all elements appear flat. We see the roof of his house, but not the walls. We also see the garage roof, the driveway, and the stone sidewalk. We see the deck behind Aaron's house as well as his vegetable garden. We also see the city street where utilities like water and electricity are located.

The front of Aaron's house faces Pleasant Street. Does your front door face the street? It doesn't have to. In many parts of the world, if the street is on the house's north side, cold winter wind can sweep inside when the door opens. In that case, you might want the door facing a different direction.

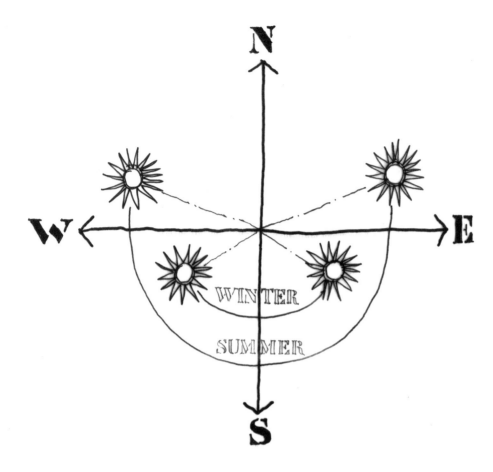

This is how the sun moves through the sky throughout the year. Think about how that might influence a building.

Generally, a room facing east gets morning light, while one facing west gets late afternoon sun and heat.

If your bedroom faced east, the sun might wake you in the morning. It would be dark at night. A kitchen on the east side would be bright and cheery for breakfast. So you see, the direction a house faces affects how we live in it. It can also affect our moods.

The direction a building faces is called the *orientation.* The site plan shows the building's orientation through use of an arrow pointing north. Generally, the north arrow points toward the top of the drawing, like on Aaron's site plan. Here are some common north arrows.

 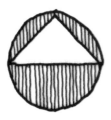 

A site plan often shows plants. This helps the architect decide which trees to keep or if new ones are needed for shade, privacy, or wind protection. This is what trees look like on a site plan.

Aaron's yard has leafy trees because he lives in the Midwest, where summers are hot, and their shade cools his house. During cold winters, the trees lose their leaves and let in warming sunlight. His trees also shelter his home from cold north winds. They reduce airborne sound and provide nesting places for birds.

Site plans also help an architect locate buildings away from things like rocks or cliffs, rivers and lakes.

Does your home have a yard? Is it different or similar to Aaron's? How do large trees make you feel? Think how the flowers smell and how their colors brighten the day. Do you like to hear birds sing? What do you like to see when you look outdoors? Is there a view of mountains, or a park, or your neighbor's yard?

The answers to these questions determine where a house is located on its site and which direction it faces. It can also influence how we live in our house.

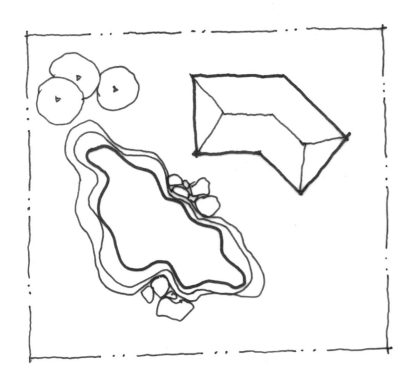

CHAPTER FOUR

The Floor Plan

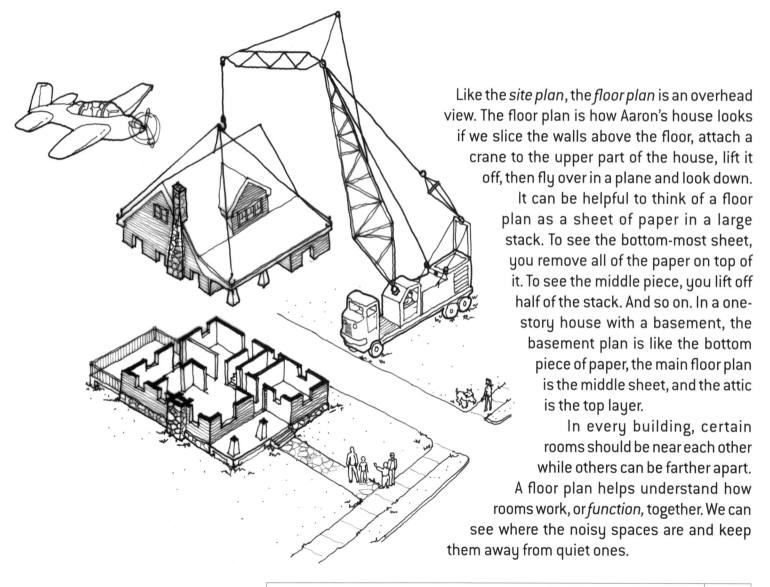

Like the *site plan*, the *floor plan* is an overhead view. The floor plan is how Aaron's house looks if we slice the walls above the floor, attach a crane to the upper part of the house, lift it off, then fly over in a plane and look down.

It can be helpful to think of a floor plan as a sheet of paper in a large stack. To see the bottom-most sheet, you remove all of the paper on top of it. To see the middle piece, you lift off half of the stack. And so on. In a one-story house with a basement, the basement plan is like the bottom piece of paper, the main floor plan is the middle sheet, and the attic is the top layer.

In every building, certain rooms should be near each other while others can be farther apart. A floor plan helps understand how rooms work, or *function,* together. We can see where the noisy spaces are and keep them away from quiet ones.

If your bedroom were located next to the kitchen, what would it be like in the morning? Would you smell bacon frying or hear dishes clinking? What would it be like if your bedroom was located next to the living room? How would your experience be different?

Before we explore Aaron's house, we need to understand how to read a floor plan. Every item in the house is represented by a specific, universal symbol. For example, walls are thick black lines, while windows divide walls and are shown as thin lines. Even pieces of furniture have symbols. Below are some common items shown *in plan.*

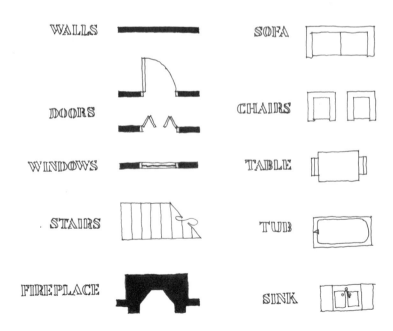

WALLS

DOORS

WINDOWS

STAIRS

FIREPLACE

SOFA

CHAIRS

TABLE

TUB

SINK

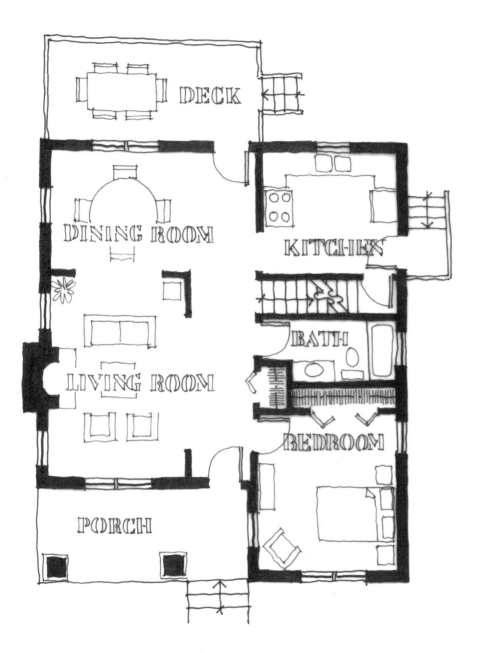

This is the floor plan for Aaron's house. Let's walk through the house room by room, starting at the front door.

Aaron's front porch faces the street. He sits outside in nice weather and chats with his neighbors. The porch also protects his front door from rain or snow, which is helpful when carrying in groceries or coming to visit.

Inside the front door is an entry hall with a coat closet. A table near the door is a good place to set keys and mail.

The living room is where Aaron entertains friends, watches television, works on his computer, and reads. Do you use your living room in as many ways as Aaron?

Imagine sitting in Aaron's living room on a winter day. The fire is roaring in the fireplace. Snow piles up outside the windows. How does it feel?

Aaron's living and dining room are located next to each other. That's handy when friends come over for dinner and a movie. There is an outdoor deck near the dining room where Aaron eats in nice weather. The dining room is also near the kitchen. Food stays hot, and crumbs and dirty dishes aren't spread all over the house.

FLOOR PLAN

The kitchen has a countertop where food is prepared. In the cabinets below and above the counter, dishes, pots, and pans are stored. Water, electricity, and gas are used for cooking and cleaning. Aaron wanted a side door near his vegetable garden and garage, as well as a door to the basement stairs. All of these requirements made designing his kitchen complicated.

Aaron's house has only one bathroom. Some houses have bathrooms on every floor for convenience. Bathrooms usually have tile floors and walls to prevent water from splattering everywhere and damaging things.

Most houses also have more than one bedroom, but since Aaron lives alone, one bedroom is enough. If his friends spend the night, they sleep on the living room sofa. Bedrooms are usually separated from entertaining areas so no one sees people in pajamas or messy beds.

Hallways and stairs are used to move from one place to the other, like a car uses a street. Stairways are vertical hallways connecting different floor levels. Aaron's stair goes down to his basement and up to his attic. On a floor plan, a stair looks like a ladder lying flat on the ground. This might help you remember how to draw stairs—we climb both ladders and stairs.

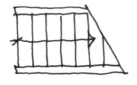
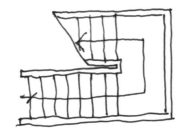

We have now explored Aaron's house. Would you change anything? Look around your home. Is your house large or small? Do you have your own room or share one with a brother or sister? What is your favorite space in your house? What makes it special? Does a room with lots of windows make you feel different from a dark one?

These are all important questions and chances are an architect asked the same questions before designing your house.

CHAPTER FIVE

Scale

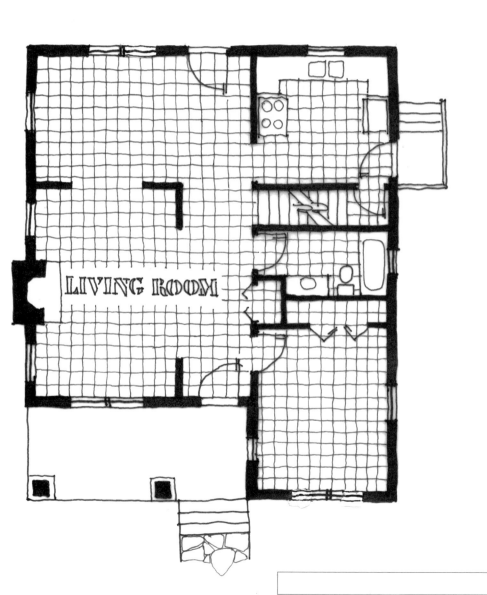

LIVING ROOM

Before we go into more detail about Aaron's house, we need to understand *scale*.

Scale is a system of measurement. It is how the size of a drawn object compares to its actual size.

A painting or a drawing is a representation of a real-life object, which might be bigger or smaller than the drawing. For example, a flower painted life-size fits on a piece of paper, but a building drawn life-size doesn't.

The construction team needs an exact image of a building to be able to build it correctly. It would be silly to have a building-sized drawing, so an architect shrinks the representation of the building to fit on a sheet of paper. This is done using *scale*.

In the United States, feet and inches are used to measure things. On an architectural drawing, each inch of a drawn line represents an actual measurement in feet on a building.

For example, let's say we want to draw a ten-foot long wall on an 8 ½" x 11" piece of paper. We could make one foot of the actual wall's length equal to one inch of the wall on our drawing. Then, the ten-foot wall shrinks to ten inches and fits on the paper.

Let's look at it another way. Imagine if you laid a tape measure against one of the walls of your living room and made a mark on the floor at every foot. If you made marks for all four walls and connected each mark to the one across the room from it, it would look like the room was sitting on a giant piece of graph paper, or a grid. This is how Aaron's floor plan would look if we made a grid on his floor.

Each side of each square of Aaron's grid represents one foot of length. There are 12 squares in one direction and 17 squares in the other. That means the room measures 12 x 17 feet. Let's look at another view of Aaron's living room.

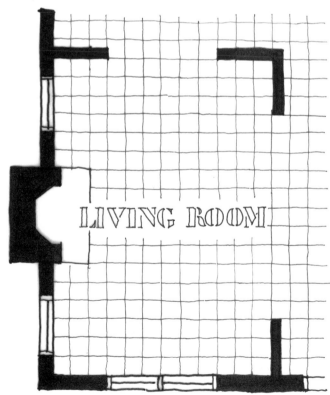

Count the number of squares. Twelve in one direction, seventeen in the other. The number of squares is the same as the previous drawing because each square represents one foot of length, but the second drawing is larger because the *scale* is larger. The big living room is easier to study than the small one.

If you look at a map of your state or country, you see it shows a large area. It may seem confusing, but a small scale is used to see a large area. On the other hand, a large scale zooms in on small areas and details to make them larger and easier to see.

Scale is always indicated on a drawing. It can be written, for example 1/8"=1'–0", ¼" = 1'-0", and so on, or shown graphically, like below.

Almost all architectural drawings are *scaled*. In fact, there is a special tool specifically designed for this purpose. It is called—can you guess?—a scale!

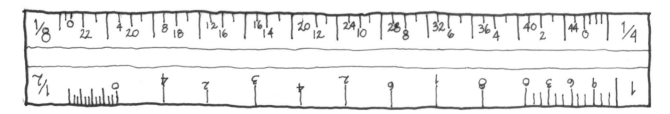

CHAPTER SIX

The Section

A floor plan is a view looking straight down, as if the walls were sliced off parallel to the floor. A *section* shows the building cut vertically from top to bottom.

Have you ever seen a dollhouse? The front face of the house swings open, allowing you to see every room on every floor simultaneously. The section is like that.

On Aaron's floor plan, solid black lines represented the walls we sliced through. On a section, the solid lines represent floors, walls, roof, and even the ground outside.

The section is an artistic tool as well as a construction aid. The section helps the architect-as-artist see the flow of space, the arrangement of openings, and their proportions. The section as a construction aid helps architect and builder understand how the building fits together.

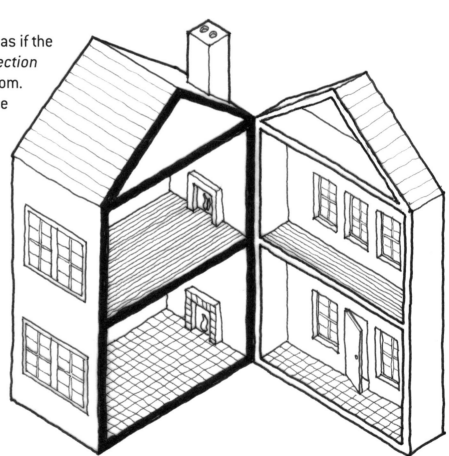

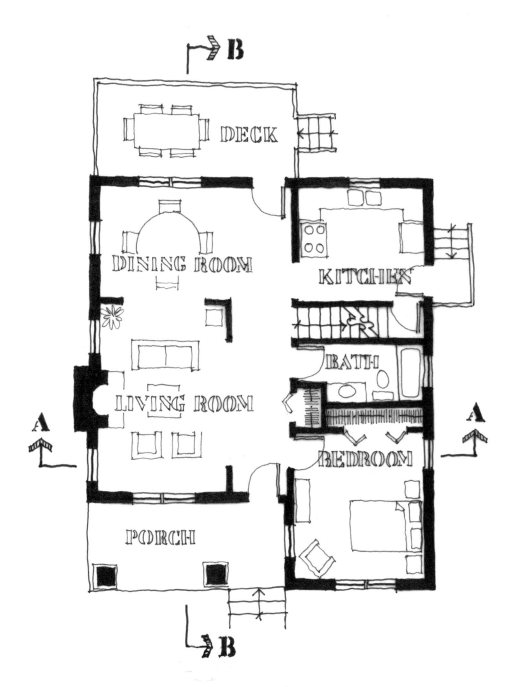

B

DECK

B

DINING ROOM

KITCHEN

LIVING ROOM

BATH

A

A

BEDROOM

PORCH

B

Look at Aaron's floor plan again. The lines labeled with the letters A and B indicate where we are cutting through Aaron's house. These lines are called, not surprisingly, section cuts. Arrows at the end of the lines show which way we are looking at the cut-apart house.

FLOOR PLAN

Section A spans from one side of Aaron's house to the other, looking toward the rear of the house. We see the living room, entry hall, and Aaron's bedroom. We see what is happening on every floor. Aaron's attic is full of stuff he is saving and his basement has the furnace and water heater in it.

Now look at section B.

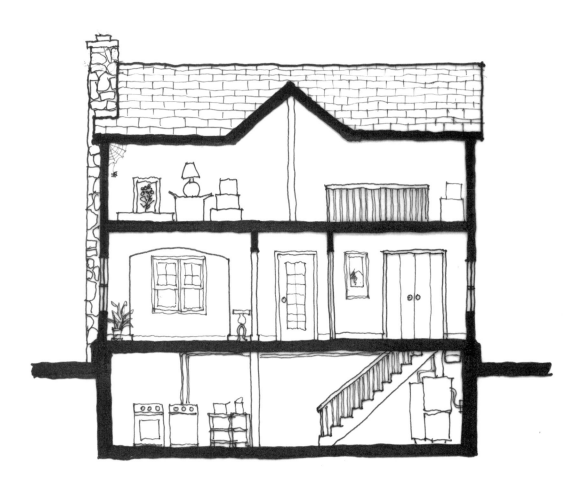

SECTION A

It's cut from front to back. We see the front porch, the living room looking toward the hall, the dining room, and deck. Changing the cutting plane changes the view of the house completely. One difference is the stairs. In section A, the stairs are shown from the side, allowing us to see how steep they are. (These are just right!) In section B, the stairs are shown from the front. They resemble a ladder like on the floor plan. Each section answers different questions about how the house is put together.

We've looked at how Aaron's house works on the inside. Now let's go outside.

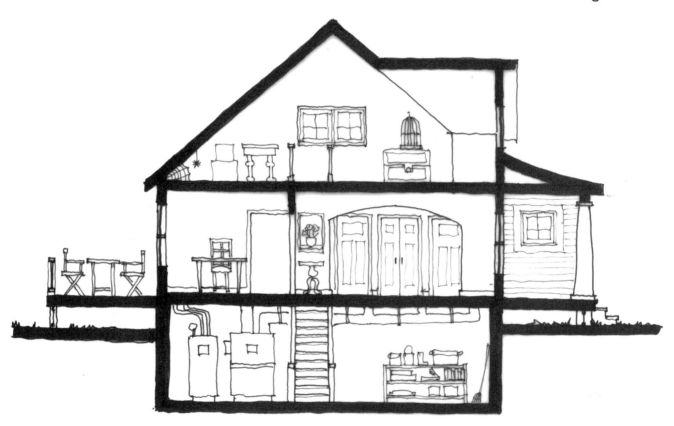

SECTION B

CHAPTER SEVEN

The Elevation

After Aaron finished his floor plan and section, it was time to design the outside of his house. To do this Aaron used an *elevation*.

The *elevation* is sometimes called a *façade*. Façade sounds like face, which is what an elevation is. It is the drawing, like a portrait, of the "face" of a building.

Imagine you are on the set of a Western movie, which is a street lined with buildings. The front of each building looks real, but if you walk behind it, there are only scaffolds holding up a flat wall.

Like the other architectural drawings, an elevation flattens the face of the building onto a sheet of paper. It helps the architect see doors and windows exactly where they occur. The architect can then decide if the windows, for example, need to be taller or a different shape or if they need to move farther from the door. It helps the architect see the overall proportion and balance. That's why it's a good building tool.

The elevation is important for another reason. Because an architect is trained in art, an elevation helps create a pleasing visual composition. The architect looks for balance, proportion, and rhythm of elements.

You have probably seen buildings you thought were beautiful, and some that weren't. Aaron has too. He tried several different "styles" of architecture to see which he preferred.

First, Aaron tried a Classical style, like the ancient Greeks and Romans...

. . .and then an International style, with lots of glass and a flat roof.

He thought the Victorian style was too fussy . . .

. . . so he tried a Prairie style.

Aaron thought it might be fun to live in a Gothic castle and pretend to be in the Middle Ages, but that wasn't appropriate for his neighborhood.

He loves the designs of the famous Spanish architect, Antoni Gaudi, but they weren't right either.

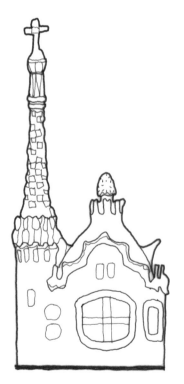

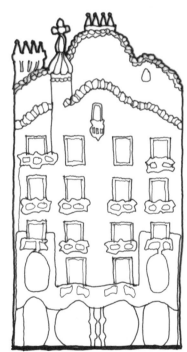

Aaron finally decided on a cottage. The word even sounds cozy, reminding Aaron of a snug fire on a cold winter day.

Most buildings have four elevations—the front, rear, and two sides. Each elevation is named for the direction it faces—north, south, east or west. Aaron's front elevation is also the south elevation.

These are the elevations of Aaron's house. Aaron's house has a gabled roof. Remember, that's two shed roofs leaning against each other like a tent. From the front, it looks like a rectangle, but from the side, it appears to be a triangle.

NORTH ELEVATION

SOUTH ELEVATION

EAST ELEVATION

Doors and windows give personality to Aaron's house. The large windows on the front porch are welcoming. His front door is made of wood and looks solid and safe. Windows in the dormer let light into the attic and make the roof seem less imposing.

Building elevations also show the materials used in construction. Aaron's house is built of wood. It has a stone fireplace. The roof is made of shingles.

WEST ELEVATION

Look at the other styles. The castle is constructed of stone. The modern house is almost all glass.

One important thing to remember about buildings is that they do not float in space, although that would be fun. Buildings sit on the ground. The ground is always shown as a big fat black line supporting the house and tying it to the earth.

CHAPTER EIGHT

Summary

The drawings for Aaron's house are now complete. Let's review how they came into being.

First, Aaron found a piece of land for his house. He studied how the sun cast shadows and which direction the wind came from. He looked at the views, the vegetation, and how people moved through the neighborhood. Taking all those things into account, he developed a *site plan*, an aerial view of his property showing the house and other improvements.

Next, Aaron created his *floor plan,* another overhead view. He moved rooms around until he found the best arrangement for his lifestyle. The *section,* a vertical cut through the building, made sure everything in the house was supported and lined up correctly. Then Aaron designed the *elevation,* giving an artistic flair and personality to the exterior of his house.

Aaron's drawings were complete, but his job wasn't over. It was time to build his house.

Aaron presented his drawings to a builder who bought the materials for the house and hired people to build it. The builder hired carpenters, stone-layers, roofers, painters, plumbers, electricians, and landscapers. They all studied Aaron's drawings to figure out each person's job.

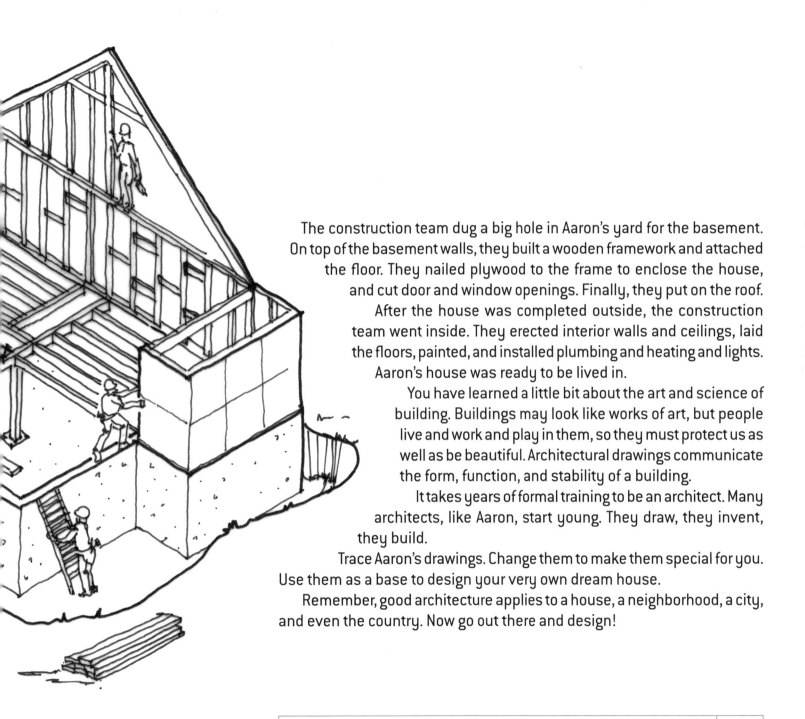

The construction team dug a big hole in Aaron's yard for the basement. On top of the basement walls, they built a wooden framework and attached the floor. They nailed plywood to the frame to enclose the house, and cut door and window openings. Finally, they put on the roof.

After the house was completed outside, the construction team went inside. They erected interior walls and ceilings, laid the floors, painted, and installed plumbing and heating and lights. Aaron's house was ready to be lived in.

You have learned a little bit about the art and science of building. Buildings may look like works of art, but people live and work and play in them, so they must protect us as well as be beautiful. Architectural drawings communicate the form, function, and stability of a building.

It takes years of formal training to be an architect. Many architects, like Aaron, start young. They draw, they invent, they build.

Trace Aaron's drawings. Change them to make them special for you. Use them as a base to design your very own dream house.

Remember, good architecture applies to a house, a neighborhood, a city, and even the country. Now go out there and design!

BIBLIOGRAPHY

Ching, Francis D.K. *Architecture: Form, Space & Order.* (New York, NY: Van Nostrand Reinhold Company, Inc., 1979)

Ching, Francis D.K. *Building Construction Illustrated.* (New York, NY: Van Nostrand Reinhold Company, Inc., 1975)

Ching, Frank. *Architectural Graphics.* (New York, NY: Van Nostrand Reinhold Company, Inc., 1975)

Dietsch, Deborah K. *Architecture for Dummies.* (Hoboken, NJ: Wiley Publishing, Inc., 2002).

Guthrie, Pat. *The Architect's Portable Handbook: First Step Rules of Thumb for Building Design.* (New York, NY: McGraw-Hill, Inc., 1995)

Kassabaum, Douglas. *Good Old Houses Neighborhood: A Book of Historic Houses to Color and Cut Out.* (Ann Arbor, MI: Educational Designs, Inc., 1981)

THE Future Architect's HANDBOOK

Barbara Beck, ARCHITECT